SLINKY INNOVATORS

The James Family

LEE SLATER

Checkerboard Library

An Imprint of Abdo Publishing
abdopublishing.com

abdopublishing.com

Published by Abdo Publishing, a division of ABDO, PO Box 398166, Minneapolis, Minnesota 55439. Copyright © 2016 by Abdo Consulting Group, Inc. International copyrights reserved in all countries. No part of this book may be reproduced in any form without written permission from the publisher. Checkerboard Library™ is a trademark and logo of Abdo Publishing.

Printed in the United States of America, North Mankato, Minnesota
102015
012016

THIS BOOK CONTAINS RECYCLED MATERIALS

Content Developer: Nancy Tuminelly
Design and Production: Mighty Media, Inc.
Series Editor: Paige Polinsky
Cover Photos: Courtesy of Tom James (center); Mighty Media (border)
Interior Photos: AP Images, p. 24, 29 (bottom right); AP Images/Corbis, p. 22; Courtesy of the Library of Congress, p. 7; Courtesy of The Strong®, Rochester, New York, pp. 12, 19, 20, 25, 27, 29 (bottom left); Courtesy of Tom James, pp. 11, 15, 23, 28 (top right); Getty Images, p. 26; iStockphoto, pp. 8, 28 (bottom left); Mighty Media, Inc., pp. 16–17; Shutterstock, pp. 5, 9, 13, 14, 16–17, 21, 29 (top left)

Library of Congress Control Number: 2015030438
Cataloging-in-Publication Data
Slater, Lee.
 Slinky innovators: the James Family / Lee Slater.
   p. cm. -- (Toy trailblazers)
ISBN 978-1-62403-979-9 (lib. bdg.)
Includes bibliographical references and index.
1. James, Richard, 1914-1974--Biography--Juvenile literature. 2. Toymakers—United States--History--Juvenile literature.
I. Title.
688.7/26/092--dc23

                              2015030438

CONTENTS

Chapter 1

RICHARD JAMES, Rookie Inventor

Richard James was born in Philadelphia, Pennsylvania, on January 1, 1914. He was six years old when the United States experienced an economic **depression**. People used the little money they had for **essential** things, such as rent, food, and clothing. Like many families, the Jameses had little money to buy toys. Yet Richard would grow up to invent the Slinky, one of the most famous toys ever!

Richard was a curious boy. He was always interested in seeing how things worked. Using his great imagination, he entertained himself by building things. His toys were tools, wires, springs, glass, wood, and broken things he could fix. Sometimes he even sold his creations!

Richard attended Westtown School, a **Quaker** boarding school in Philadelphia. His time in school

FUN FACT

Slinky is the official state toy of Pennsylvania.

In 2015, Pennsylvania State University was ranked the twenty-fifth best engineering school in the nation.

helped him become a professional problem solver. When it was time to go to college, he knew exactly what he wanted to be.

Richard studied **mechanical engineering** at Pennsylvania State University. He graduated in 1939. Now people would pay him to build, fix, and invent things! Richard soon took a job as a **naval engineer**. He spent his days designing and building parts for ships.

Chapter 2

The War EFFORT

While Richard was at Penn State, he met a young woman named Betty Mattas. Betty was born in Altoona, Pennsylvania, on February 13, 1918. She was the only child of Clair and Irene Mattas. In 1940, Richard and Betty were married.

Just one year later, the United States joined **World War II**. Men and women who were not fighting supported the armed forces in other ways. They worked in factories making **ammunition**, uniforms, airplanes, tanks, and ships. Richard wanted to help the United States. He took a job that would contribute to the **war effort**.

Richard worked at William Cramp & Sons Shipbuilding Company in Philadelphia. The company had a contract with the US government. Its workers built submarines, ocean tugboats, and floating workshops. William Cramp & Sons needed plenty of designers, engineers, and builders. During the war, more than 10,000 people worked at the company!

The William Cramp & Sons shipyard thrived in the early 1940s.

Engineers like Richard were always working to solve problems. One problem was that rough seas often broke sensitive **nautical** instruments. Ships and submarines used these instruments to navigate, communicate, and locate enemies. The lives of the people on board depended on these resources.

The engineers needed to stabilize these instruments. That way, the instruments could work in rough conditions. While Richard tried to solve the problem, a happy accident occurred.

Chapter 3

The Happy ACCIDENT

Richard tried to stabilize the ship's instruments with springs. One day in 1943, he knocked a spring off his desk. He watched as the coil of wire tumbled across the floor. The spring almost looked as if it were walking

One clumsy bump changed toy history!

across the room. He thought that kids could have a lot of fun with something like this! Maybe Richard was thinking about toys because he had a new baby. His first son, Tom, had been born that year.

Richard thought about the tumbling spring all day long. He could hardly wait to tell Betty about his idea. When he got home, he told her, "I think I can make a toy out of this!"

Richard worked on his invention over the next year. He knew that the right wire and **tension** would make the toy walk. But first he had to solve many problems. What type of wire would give the toy the right bounce? How would the wire stretch and spring back to its original shape? How many coils of wire should the toy have? What kind of machine would he need to manufacture it? If anyone could answer these questions, Richard could!

Chapter 4

SLINKY IS BORN!

Finally, in early 1944, Richard was satisfied with his invention. It worked exactly the way he had imagined. But now he had to see if kids would like it.

Before a new product is **mass-produced**, the inventor usually does some **market** research. He or she needs to know if people will like and buy the product. Richard was ready to do his market research. He looked close to home for kids to test his toy.

Richard's son Tom gave the new toy a try. Richard also showed the toy to kids in the neighborhood. They loved it! It walked right down stairs. It was also fun to toss the toy from hand to hand. Since the neighbor kids liked the toy, Richard knew other kids would like it too.

Before Richard and Betty could sell the toy, it needed a name. Betty began looking through a dictionary to find the right word. She searched for two days. Then she found it! The word *slinky* means sleek and graceful. That **definition**

FUN FACT

It takes 80 feet (24.4 m) of wire to make one Slinky.

perfectly fit the sound and movement of the toy.

Richard and Betty created the James Spring and Wire Company. The couple borrowed $500 and bought enough wire to make hundreds of Slinky toys. Richard and Betty were in business!

Chapter 5

SLINKY HITS
the Stores

In 1945, Richard and Betty decided to introduce Slinky to the public. They visited local toy stores and showed Slinky to the owners. But the store owners did not share Richard and Betty's enthusiasm.

Some toy store owners thought the Slinky didn't look as colorful or exciting as other toys.

FUN FACT

Today, some Slinkys are available in silver-coated metal and plated with 14-karat gold!

Slinky didn't look very exciting. It was just a gray coil of wire in a plain paper wrapper. The store owners didn't think it would sell. Richard and Betty were disappointed, but they kept trying.

Then Gimbels, a huge department store in Philadelphia, decided to take a chance. They bought 400 Slinkys for the Christmas season. Richard and Betty were excited, but the Slinkys looked boring sitting on a shelf. Shoppers needed to see it in action!

Richard called Betty and told her to meet him at Gimbels in a few hours. Then he went to the toy department. He set up a wooden ramp on a table. Then he demonstrated how Slinky could walk. The display was a hit! By the time Betty arrived, all 400 Slinkys had been sold. And by that Christmas, the James family had sold 22,000 Slinkys!

Chapter 6

THE BUSINESS
Takes Off

The American International Toy Fair takes place every year in New York City. Toy buyers from all over the country come to see the newest toys. In 1946, Slinky made its **debut** at the fair. Richard demonstrated Slinky and gave his sales pitch. The crowd loved it! Buyers for department stores and toy stores lined up to order Slinkys. The toy was a national sensation by the end of the year.

After the fair, Richard couldn't make the Slinkys fast enough. So he invented a machine that made the production process faster. It could make a Slinky in less than five seconds! He placed the machine in his grandfather's pattern shop in Philadelphia's Germantown neighborhood. But the **demand** for Slinkys kept rising. Before long, Richard opened a factory in the Clifton Heights neighborhood of Philadelphia.

Slinky continued to grow more and more famous. It was recognized around the world. Within a couple of years, more than 100 million Slinkys

FUN FACT

More than 300 million Slinky
toys have been sold since 1946.

had been sold. Richard's simple invention had earned his family millions of dollars!

Soon, more toys joined the Slinky family. A smaller version, Slinky Jr., was created in 1948. And in 1952, Slinky Dog arrived. Its head and rear end were plastic, but its body was a Slinky. It was a hit!

By the late 1940s, toy stores no longer hesitated to put Slinkys on display.

Chapter 7

LIFE OF A SLINKY

Richard's engineering skills greatly improved the Slinky-making process. In fact, the machine he invented is still used to make today's Slinkys! There are five main steps to making a Slinky.

1 A worker feeds high-carbon steel wire into the machine.

2 The machine flattens the wire and winds it around a metal **cylinder**. The machine automatically cuts the wire after wrapping 98 coils around the cylinder.

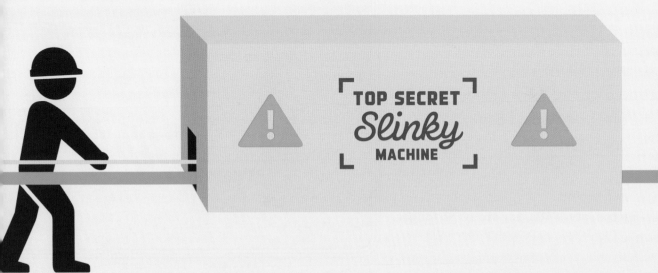

TOP SECRET
Slinky
MACHINE

3 Another worker removes the Slinky from the machine. He or she **crimps** each end to the coil next to it.

4 The Slinky is packaged in a box. The box will later be wrapped with plastic.

5 Workers place the individual boxes in larger boxes for shipping. The Slinkys begin their journey to stores around the world!

Chapter 8

RICHARD
Moves On

In 1956, the company's name changed to James Industries. Richard and Betty were very wealthy. They had six children and a wildly successful business. They lived in a huge home in the wealthy Bryn Mawr **suburb** of Philadelphia. But everything wasn't going as well as it seemed.

Sometimes it is difficult for people to adjust to fame. Richard was not comfortable with his invention's success. He withdrew from his family and friends. He also secretly **donated** millions of dollars to religious charities.

One day, Richard shocked Betty by telling her he was moving to South America. He wanted Betty and the children to move to Bolivia with him. But Betty always thought of their children first. The children were happy in their

FUN FACT

Slinky is on display at the Smithsonian Institution in Washington, DC, and in the Metropolitan Museum of Art in New York City.

Popular toys like Slinky train brought fame and fortune to the James family.

comfortable home. They had friends, activities, and schools they liked. Going to South America would unsettle their lives.

Richard decided to go to Bolivia on his own. In 1960, he bought a one-way ticket and left his family. Betty had to take charge of the family and the business. But Richard's **donations** had burdened the business with **debt**. Betty had a big challenge ahead of her.

Chapter 9

MOM, PRESIDENT, Reinventor

Betty was suddenly a single parent and company president. And the company was in financial trouble. Betty had to turn the business around. If she did not, she and the children could lose their house.

Slinky Dog's impressive sales aided James Industries during its financial crisis.

FUN FACT

Slinky was selected as one of the All-TIME 100 Greatest Toys by *TIME* magazine.

Betty was determined to save her home and make the business successful again. First, she arranged to pay the creditors back in small amounts. Then she moved the factory to Hollidaysburg, Pennsylvania. This way it was closer to home. A caregiver helped tend the children while Betty worked.

Slinky Dog helped Betty keep the business afloat. The toy had been a great success during the 1950s. It was still very popular and sold well.

But profits weren't the only thing that mattered. Betty believed it was important to keep Slinky affordable. She felt a commitment to children whose families couldn't afford expensive toys. The price stayed low, and the company sold millions of Slinkys. James Industries had officially bounced back!

Richard did not return to the company or his family. In 1974, he died in Bolivia. He was 60 years old.

Chapter 10

THE FAMOUS Slinky Jingle

Betty once told a reporter, "The simplicity of Slinky is what made it so successful." But it wasn't just simplicity that made Slinky successful. Good advertising helped a lot!

In 1962, Betty decided to advertise Slinky on television. It was easier to sell Slinky when people could see it in action. She hired musicians to write a **jingle** for the commercial.

Betty's plan was a smart **marketing** decision. A good jingle is hard to forget. You might find yourself humming or singing it over and over.

The Slinky commercial showed that a spring is a marvelous thing!

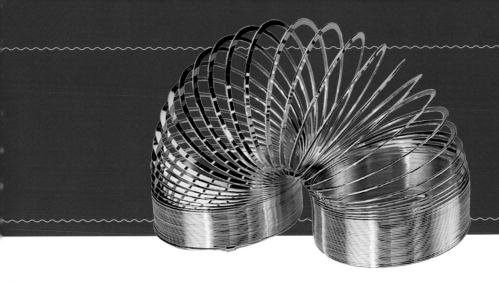

Jingles were first used to sell products during radio shows. On television, jingles could be used with images too. They were an effective form of advertising.

The Slinky jingle **debuted** in a television ad in 1963. It was the longest-running jingle in television history. If you ask your grandparents to sing it, they probably can!

Over the years, the jingle's words changed to appeal to new generations of children. New Slinky jingles aired during the 1970s and 1980s. Today, the jingle isn't on television anymore. But Slinkys continue to be simple, sensational, and fun for everyone!

THE SLINKY JINGLE

Everyone knows it's Slinky!

What walks down stairs
alone or in pairs
and makes a slinkity sound?

A spring, a spring,
a marvelous thing,
everyone knows it's Slinky!

It's Slinky, it's Slinky,
for fun, it's a wonderful toy.

It's Slinky, it's Slinky,
it's fun for a girl and a boy.

It's fun for a girl and a boy.

Chapter 11

SLINKY
Fame & Fortune

Betty was a **marketing whiz!** She kept Slinkys exciting by releasing new versions. These included Slinky Pets, plastic Slinky, and Crazy Eyes glasses. The new toys gave **consumers** more Slinky products to buy. As sales grew, so did the company.

In 1995, Walt Disney Pictures contacted Betty. They were creating a movie called *Toy Story*. One of the characters was a talking Slinky Dog. Betty was very excited! She had her designers change the Slinky Dog to match the one in *Toy Story*. In the first year after the movie's release, nearly 1 million Slinky Dogs were sold.

Betty James plays with the toy that launched her empire.

Betty often got offers from companies who wanted to buy James Industries. But she wasn't going to sell until she was ready. It was fun running a successful company! The 120 employees were almost like family to Betty.

Only one of the six James children went into the family business. The oldest, Tom, became the sales manager. He worked at the company headquarters with his mother.

In 1998, Betty was finally ready to retire. She sold the Slinky brand to Poof Products, Inc. Betty lived another 10 years to enjoy her success. On November 20, 2008, she died at the age of 90. Her family had grown to include 16 grandchildren and two great-grandchildren.

Chapter 12

SLINKY
Moves Forward

Hundreds of millions of Slinkys have been sold since its invention. It has been popular for so long that it is called a classic toy.

But Slinky is more than a toy! People have found all kinds of creative uses for it. Teachers use Slinky to demonstrate **physics**.

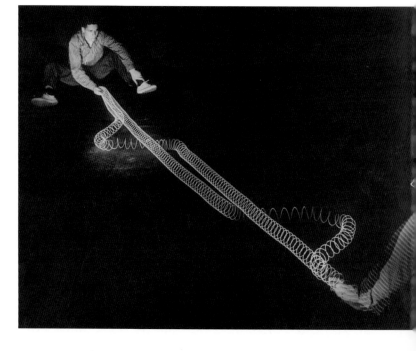

Scientists at the Massachusetts Institute of Technology use Slinkys to teach physics.

In the 1990s, James Industries released a Slinky telephone!

Astronauts used Slinky for experiments on board the space shuttle *Discovery*. They wanted to study the effects of **zero gravity** on springs.

United States troops used Slinkys as radio antennas during the **Vietnam War**. Today, they are used in machines that pick pecans. Some people use them to tie back curtains. Slinky can even keep squirrels away from birdhouses!

Whether walking down stairs or going to space, Slinky shows no sign of slowing down. It is one of the best-selling and most famous toys of all time. And it all started with a happy accident!

TIMELINE

1914

Richard James is born in Philadelphia, Pennsylvania, on January 1.

1918

Betty Mattas is born in Altoona, Pennsylvania, on February 13.

1940

Richard and Betty are married.

1943

Richard gets the idea to make a spring into a toy.

1946

Slinky debuts at the American International Toy Fair in New York City.

FUN FACT

In 1999, the US Postal Service honored Slinky on a stamp.

33 USA — Slinky Craze Begins 1945

1974

Richard dies at age 60.

1998

Betty sells the Slinky brand to Poof Products, Inc. Betty retires.

1960

Richard moves to Bolivia. Betty becomes president of James Industries.

1995

Toy Story inspires a redesigned Slinky Dog.

2008

Betty dies on November 20.

Glossary

ammunition – things such as bullets or shells that can be fired from weapons.

consumer – a person who buys and uses products and services.

crimp – to cause to become wavy, bent, or pinched.

cylinder – a solid, round shape with flat ends. A soda can is a cylinder.

debt – the condition of owing money or something else to someone.

debut – a first appearance. To debut something is to present or perform it for the first time.

definition – the meaning of a word.

demand – the amount of an available product that buyers are willing and able to purchase.

depression – a time when the economy of a country is shrinking and many people lose their jobs.

donate – to give.

essential – necessary or very important.

jingle – a short song with memorable words designed to sell a product or service.

market – a particular type of people who might buy something. Marketing is the process of advertising or promoting something so people will want to buy it.

mass-produce – to use machines to make large amounts of identical things in a factory.

mechanical engineering – the science or profession of designing and building machines or engines.

nautical – related to sailors, navigation, or ships.

naval engineer – someone who is specially trained to design and build ships, boats, or other marine structures.

physics – the science of how energy and objects affect each other.

Quaker – of or relating to the Society of Friends, a Christian group that prefers simple religious services and opposes war.

suburb – a town, village, or community just outside a city.

tension – the stiffness or tightness of something such as rope or wire.

Vietnam War – from 1957 to 1975. A long, failed attempt by the United States to stop North Vietnam from taking over South Vietnam.

war effort – a coordinated gathering of resources during wartime.

whiz – a person who has great skill or ability in a particular field or activity.

World War II – from 1939 to 1945, fought in Europe, Asia, and Africa. Great Britain, France, the United States, the Soviet Union, and their allies were on one side. Germany, Italy, Japan, and their allies were on the other side.

zero gravity – the absence of weight, as in outer space.